A SIMPLE GUIDE TO GETTING INTO COLLEGE

2014 - 2015 EDITION

NO LONGER THE PROPERTY OF
BOYNTON BEACH CITY LIBRARY

Heather Case

LUMINIS BOOKS
Published by Luminis Books
1950 East Greyhound Pass, #18, PMB 280,
Carmel, Indiana, 46033, U.S.A.
Copyright © Luminis Books, 2014

PUBLISHER'S NOTICE

The Publisher and Author make no warranties or representations regarding the accuracy or completeness of this work and disclaim all warranties, including without limitation warranties of fitness for a particular purpose. The information contained in this guide may not be suitable for every situation, and the Publisher is not engaged in providing legal, accounting, or other professional services. Some information and links on the Internet change frequently. The Publisher is not responsible for content on third party websites referenced in this work and does not endorse any organization or information provided on such sites. Neither the Publisher nor Author shall be liable for damages arising herefrom.

Cover art direction and design by Brit Godish. Cover photograph courtesy of Shutterstock.

ISBN-13: 978-1-935462-05-7
Printed in the United States of America

10 9 8 7 6 5 4 3 2 1

Simple Guides

give you

Just the Facts

Get up to speed on Getting into College fast!

Simple Guides: get you started quickly.

No extra clutter, no extra reading.

Learn how to get started with finding the right college for you, then find out how to ace college admissions tests, create a list of colleges you want to apply to, line up financial aid, schedule campus visits, complete the apps to the colleges you like, write an exceptional essay, and get in to the college you want!

Table of Contents

Introduction	1
Chapter 1 – What Are Colleges Looking For?	3
Chapter 2 – College Admissions Tests	21
Chapter 3 – Creating Your List	41
Chapter 4 – The Application	72
Chapter 5 – Essays and Interviews	103
Conclusion	113

INTRODUCTION

The higher education system in the United States is the only one in the world that evaluates students' applications on more than test scores and grades. It is full of schools of all sizes and persuasion with seemingly endless possibilities for undergraduate studies. However, because the application process varies from one school to another, it can be difficult to know how and when to begin the application process. Regardless of how exciting it can be to think about going to college, actually applying can be incredibly stressful.

All of the well-meaning people in your life have an opinion about where you should apply. Your parents, friends, counselors, teachers all have ideas about what you should do and how you should do it. But, your parents applied to college in a different decade. Your friends may not have the same needs for a post-secondary education. Your counselors and teachers may have helped hundreds, maybe even thousands of students before you, but they may not know you as well as your parents and friends. You are probably ready to bury your head in the sand and hope that somehow you will just "get in." However, the chances of that happening are about as good as winning the lottery when you haven't purchased a ticket.

Don't distress. This simple guide is designed to help you manage this complicated process with clear, concise steps and activities. After reading these five chapters, you will be able to:

- ✓ Understand the most recent trends in the college admissions process
- ✓ Identify schools that best meet your strengths and needs for post-secondary education
- ✓ Complete all of your college applications and supplements
- ✓ Write a killer essay

For those students, parents, or counselors who want more detail about the information provided in this book, supplemental material is available in video format through www.udemy.com and can be easily located by searching for "SGTGI." There are many different options available so that students may tailor their learning to their specific needs. Some of the "SGTGI" content is free and some requires a registration fee. For more information about this resource, please see "Other Services" at the end of the book.

CHAPTER 1: WHAT ARE COLLEGES LOOKING FOR?

KEY TERMS

With more than 4,300 colleges and universities in the United States, there is something for everyone, literally. There are schools that boast acceptance rates of less than 10 percent, with some of the smallest acceptance rates hovering around five percent. There are also schools with open enrollment policies which allow them to admit anyone with a high school diploma or GED. There are research schools, liberal arts schools, land-grant universities, conservatories, and countless other types of degree granting institutions. So let's start there, with definitions. This list will focus on undergraduate studies that result in a four-year degree.

COLLEGE VS. UNIVERSITY

In the United States, the term college and university are often used interchangeably. This is not true, however, in other parts of the world. There are some general differences that exist in the format of the two entities, but generally speaking there is not a significant difference in the academic meaning of the word when referring to post-secondary schools in the United States. The major difference between a college and a university is the way in which the majors are arranged.

Graduates from colleges all receive a degree granted by the college, regardless of the major. Universities, on the other hand, are arranged by "schools" within the University. These "schools" are comprised within disciplines and when combined make up the university.

Perhaps the most common misconception is that Universities are large institutions and colleges are small. This is not necessarily the case.

Types of Undergraduate Degrees:

BA – Bachelor of Arts - The curriculum of the BA degree is generally focused in the "arts." Majors, and therefore a majority of the coursework, is completed in the humanities, social sciences, or fine arts. In many post-secondary schools two years of a foreign language are required to complete a BA degree.

BFA – Bachelor of Fine Arts - The curriculum of the BFA degree is generally focused on the fine or performing arts. Majors, and therefore a majority of the coursework, is completed in the "studio" of the particular discipline in contrast to the traditional classroom which comprises the other Bachelor's degrees. A BFA may be awarded in a wide variety of disciplines such as art, creative writing, dance, drama/theater, music (vocal or instrumental), or television production.

BS – Bachelor of Science - The curriculum of the BS degree is generally focused in the "sciences." Majors, and therefore a majority of the coursework, is completed in the natural/life sciences, physical sciences, or mathematics.

TYPES OF SCHOOLS:

For-Profit – Colleges and universities that exist to provide not only education services to students but also to provide a financial benefit to their stock holders or investors. These schools generally have one tuition rate regardless of residence (within the United States).

Private – Colleges and universities that do not receive state funding and rely on independent sources for funding are considered private schools. Some are religiously affiliated, some may have been founded by a religious institution but no longer maintain the religious affiliation, and some may have been started by a specific group with a specific purpose. These schools also generally have one tuition rate regardless of residence (within the United States) and are non-profit entities.

Public – Colleges and universities that receive funding from state governments are considered state universities. Generally these schools have a lower tuition for in-state residents because they receive funding from the state government. These are also non-profit entities.

TYPES OF INSTITUTIONAL FOCUS:

Art Colleges and Conservatories – These institutions focus on preparing students for art-related careers. Conservatories generally focus on performance-based majors while arts schools focus on the visual arts and related careers. In some arts schools the only degree you can earn is a "fine arts" (BFA, MFA) degree.

Land Grant – These institutions were established through the Land Grant Acts in the 1800s. These Acts gave federal land to states to establish colleges which would be accessible to all and would provide an educational focus in agricultural and technical areas. Two of the most selective land grant schools are Cornell and MIT. However, there is at least one land grant school in every state:

http://congress.indiana.edu/morrill-land-grant-college-act

Liberal Arts – These institutions generally focus on exposing students to a wide variety of curriculum and often have a "core" curriculum which is required to graduate. Coursework often focuses on the interconnection between divisions and schools.

Research – These institutions generally focus on providing an environment where cutting-edge research can occur.

THINGS TO CONSIDER

With so many different types of post-secondary education available, it would seem that each school would be looking for a different type of student. However, there are many things that all institutions are looking for in prospective students. The National Association for College Admissions Counseling (NACAC) has collected data from the admissions offices across the country for the past eleven years. They reported their findings in the 2013 S*tate of College Admission:*

http://www.nacacnet.org/media-center/PressRoom/2014/Pages/SOCA2013.aspx

In this report they listed the top ten things that colleges cites as critical in application review. They are, in order:

1. Grades in college prep courses
2. Strength of curriculum
3. Admission test scores
4. Grades in all courses
5. Essay or writing sample
6. Student's demonstrated interest
7. Counselor recommendation
8. Teacher recommendation

9. Class rank
10. Extracurricular activities

There are many things you can take away from this data. First, grades in college prep courses is the single most important factor of a college application. The thing students most often overlook is the fact that many colleges make their "yes" or "no" decisions based on grades through the end of the junior year. Some schools have the benefit of having first semester grades from the senior year, but many applications are processed before those grades are even available. That means that by the end of the first semester of 10th grade half of all of the grades a college will see are already finalized. HALF! Too often students think, "I'll do better next year," or "I'm only a freshman, so my grades don't really matter yet." That type of thinking couldn't be further from the truth. Every grade in every class beginning with the first day of ninth grade counts.

The only exception to this rule is the University of California (UC) system, but then the UC schools have an application unlike anyone else. For example, they ask students to self-report grades beginning in 10th grade. If a student is admitted, he is required to submit an official transcript to verify the information provided in the application. Additionally, the UC system only accepts applications from November 1 to November 30 of any given year for fall admission. Students must apply to each campus individually during the 30-day application period to be considered for admission. Late applications are not accepted:

http://admission.universityofcalifornia.edu/how-to-apply/dates-deadlines/index.html

So, maybe you're thinking that you should just take a bunch of easy courses and get A's. Right? Unfortunately, it isn't that easy. The second most significant thing on your application is the strength of curriculum. This refers to the difficulty of the courses a student takes. High schools are asked to send a "school profile" with student applications. These profiles include data about the school like college matriculation rate, average SAT/ACT scores, and curriculum offerings. Colleges and universities use this information to put student applications into perspective. For example, one of the criteria many colleges and universities use to evaluate the strength of student's curriculum in terms of the number of Honors, Advanced Placement (AP) or International Baccalaureate (IB) courses completed. If high school "A" only offers three AP courses, but high school "B" offers 15, it isn't fair to hold a student from high school "A" to the same standard regarding number of AP/IB courses as student from high school "B."

In a different but related vein, it is important to note that taking a bunch of AP courses and getting B's or lower is not a great plan either. Too often students insist on taking as many AP/IB courses as their schedule can hold, which often results in lower performance. B's do not impress colleges. C's of any kind, but especially in AP courses are a red flag that a student may not be ready to handle the rigor and responsibility of college level course work. A strong transcript is one which has predominantly A's – even if that means that there are only one or two AP courses. When choosing which AP courses to take, consider what classes you enjoy the most and which ones come most naturally to you, and take AP courses in those subjects. If you hate science then don't take AP Biology. Consider instead AP courses in the humanities.

To underscore this point further, you need only consider that colleges are looking for passionate students. They are no longer interested in the well-rounded, jack-of-all-trades-master-of-none student. They want students who have discovered a passion and have pursued that passion as far as possible within the context of the offerings that are reasonably available within their high schools and greater community.

If science or engineering is your passion, take all of the AP science courses offered at your school and do very well in them. Complete a research project and present it at your local or regional science and engineering fair. Schedule a time to shadow an engineer or a doctor or schedule an internship of some kind over the summer before your senior year.

If you can't live without music or the performing arts, take all of the music or drama courses your school offers and find ways to play/perform in your community through youth symphonies, choirs, or civic theaters. Take dual credit music courses at a local college or university if your school has limited performing arts offerings.

If social sciences or humanities is what you love best, take AP courses in psychology, economics, literature, a foreign language, or history. Choose extracurricular activities that will help you explore these areas and strengthen your skills such as speech and debate, Model UN, or a writing club.

After you have found your passion and have explored it for yourself, find ways to share the skills you have developed by taking on leadership roles within your clubs or organizations, or by volunteering in the greater community in a role that is tied to your interest. When you share what you love your enthusiasm and excitement will be evident and those around you will have wonderful things to say about your commitment and zeal. You may find their opinions invaluable when you need letters of recommendation.

Finding your passion doesn't necessarily mean that you will major in that area in college. For many students this does prove to be true. However, it is not so much the area of your passion that impresses colleges but rather the fact that you are so excited about a particular area of interest that you develop the time management skills and demonstrate dedication and follow-through to foster your interest in something that is important to you. If you aren't sure what you want to major in, but you love horses then find ways to learn everything you can about horses and be involved with horses.

Finally, it is important to note that the college admissions landscape is ever changing. For example, student's demonstrated interest is listed as the sixth most important part of the college application in this report. Today it is more important than your counselor and teacher letters, but in 2002 it wasn't even on the list. Colleges are receiving record numbers of applications. In fact, UCLA set a new record with well over 90,000 fall 2013 applications, and then broke their own record in 2014 with more than 100,000 applications for fall admission:

http://thechoice.blogs.nytimes.com/2013/01/28/college-application-tally-2013/

http://dailybruin.com/2014/01/17/ucla-sets-records-with-more-than-100000-fall-2014-applicants/

As a result of ever increasing numbers of applications, institutions are trying to figure out who is most likely to enroll if accepted. As a result, many are tracking demonstrated interest. This means that they pay attention to which students visit the campus, and which students reply to emails from the college or university, and what students attend info sessions or other college-sponsored events.

While it is increasingly clear that no two schools are tracking student interest in exactly the same way, it is important to understand the wide variety of responses you will find within post-secondary institutions. Some colleges are paying such close attention to a student's demonstrated interest that an admissions representative knows exactly how many emails the student has received, which ones he opened, and how he responded to each email that he did open. While on the other hand, some schools openly admit that they do not even consider demonstrated interest until they begin evaluating students on the wait list. Regardless of the school's position on demonstrated interest, there are some things you can begin doing now which will help you to show your prospective colleges that you are interested.

1. Visit the campus whenever possible. Before you go, be sure to schedule yourself for an official tour and info session. When you arrive on

campus, be sure you sign in with the admissions office so that they know you were there.
2. Take a virtual tour (yes, some colleges are tracking your interaction with their web page).
3. Sign up for the mailing list.
4. Be sure to check your email regularly and open and respond to the emails from the colleges that you are considering.
5. Attend a college fair and stop by the booth – again be sure to fill out their card or sign in on the list so that you get credit for being there. Better yet, actually wait in line to talk to the admissions rep at the fair.
6. If the college visits your school be sure to sign up for the info session and attend. Again, fill out a card or sign in!

IN REVIEW

- ✓ Understand that there are thousands of schools with many different options for all types of students.
- ✓ Take the most challenging courses that you can do well in.
- ✓ Find ways to connect with the colleges and universities you are considering.

NEXT STEPS

Take a few moments to complete the forms below so that you are able to organize all of your application assets in one place, Doing so will let you know not only what you are currently doing well, but may also allow you to recognize some areas where you may need to work harder or add new opportunities to fill in any holes you may discover.

Additionally, it is important to make note of new things as you add them. Many of things listed on this inventory will become a part of your college applications and it will make the process of applying much easier because you will have all of this information in one place when you begin completing applications in your senior year. It is much easier to keep track of things as you complete them than it is to try to recall activities or grades you completed several months or years ago.

Academic – Grades & Rigor of Curriculum

9th Grade Grades in College Preparatory Classes (English, Math, Science, Social Sciences & Languages):

Semester 1 Classes	Grade	Type	Semester 2 Classes	Grade	Type

Type of course:
R = Regular   H = Honors   A = Accelerated
AP = Advanced Placement
IB = International Baccalaureate   DC = Dual Credit

10th Grade Grades in College Preparatory Classes (English, Math, Science, Social Sciences & Languages):

Semester 1 Classes	Grade	Type	Semester 2 Classes	Grade	Type

Type of course:
R = Regular   H = Honors   A = Accelerated
AP = Advanced Placement
IB = International Baccalaureate   DC = Dual Credit

11th Grade Grades in College Preparatory Classes (English, Math, Science, Social Sciences & Languages):

Semester 1 Classes	Grade	Type	Semester 2 Classes	Grade	Type

Type of course:
R = Regular   H = Honors   A = Accelerated
AP = Advanced Placement
IB = International Baccalaureate   DC = Dual Credit

12th Grade Schedule of College Preparatory Classes (English, Math, Science, Social Sciences & Languages):

Semester 1 Classes	Type	Semester 2 Classes	Type

Type of course:
R = Regular   H = Honors   A = Accelerated
AP = Advanced Placement
IB = International Baccalaureate   DC = Dual Credit

Extracurricular Activities

Consider academic, athletic, fine art, or other clubs and activities in which you participated in grades 9 – 12. After you have completed your list, have your parents or a close friend review it to be sure you have not forgotten anything.

Activity	Grades Participated	Positions Held	Awards & Recognition

CHAPTER 2: COLLEGE ADMISSIONS TESTS

KEY TERMS

Whether you like it or not, college admissions tests play a significant role in the application process for many colleges. However, not all tests are intended to measure the same things. Some tests cover acquired knowledge while others test ability to learn. It is important to understand the key differences in the critical tests as you begin to plan your strategy for test-taking.

TYPES OF TESTS:

ACT (www.actstudent.org)

The ACT is an achievement test which means it tests what you already know:

http://www.act.org/research/policymakers/pdf/best_testprep.pdf

Some important facts about the ACT:

- ✓ The ACT is scored 1 – 36 in four content areas: English, Math, Reading, and Science.
- ✓ ACT Math tests algebra, geometry, algebra II, and trigonometry.

- ✓ The composite score is an average of the scores in the four content areas.
- ✓ There is NO point deduction for wrong answers.
- ✓ There are six test dates per school year (September – June).

SAT (www.collegeboard.com)

The SAT is a critical reasoning test. It tests not only what you know but how well you can apply that information to new scenarios:

http://sat.collegeboard.org/about-tests/sat

Some important facts about the SAT:

- ✓ The SAT is scored 200 – 800 in three content areas: Critical Reading, Math, and Writing.
- ✓ Most colleges use only the Critical Reading and Math scores for admissions purposes.
- ✓ SAT Math tests algebra, geometry, and algebra II.
- ✓ There IS a ¼ point deduction for each wrong answer (guessing penalty).
- ✓ There are six test dates per school year (September – June).
- ✓ It is important to note that the College Board recently announced that it will be revising the SAT http://www.insidehighered.com/news/2013/02/27/college-board-announces-plans-redesign-

sat. While this sounds very exciting, these changes will not be in effect for those students applying in 2014. In fact, with the last revision of the SAT the announcement preceded the new test by years. Students in high school today will still have to choose between the current SAT and the ACT.

SAT Subject Tests (www.collegeboard.com)

The SAT Subject Tests are content-specific tests. Many selective or highly-selective schools require them as a part of the application for admission. Each test is scored 200 – 800 and lasts about one hour. Students can take up to three subject tests on the same day. However, a student can only take the SAT or the SAT Subject Tests (not both) on a given test date, and not all subject tests are offered on all of the test dates.

For the 2013 - 2014 School year Subject Tests will be given in the following areas:

- Literature
- U.S. History
- World History
- Math Level 1
- Math Level 2
- Biology/EM
- Chemistry
- Physics
- French
- French with Listening
- German
- German with Listening
- Spanish
- Spanish with Listening
- Modern Hebrew
- Italian
- Latin
- Chinese with Listening
- Japanese with Listening
- Korean with Listening

For additional information about what each subject test covers and to see sample problems, visit:

http://sat.collegeboard.org/about-tests/sat-subject-tests.

AP and IB Exams

Advanced Placement (AP) and International Baccalaureate (IB) exams are usually taken after a student completes the corresponding AP or IB exam. These scores are not required for college applications, but if a student scores extremely well on an AP exam it might be mentioned in a counselor or teacher letter. At some colleges students may earn college credit for AP/IB scores that are high enough. For more information about these two programs, see the links below:

IB Programme - https://ibanswers.ibo.org/

AP Courses –

https://apstudent.collegeboard.org/exploreap

English Proficiency Tests (for International Students)

TOEFL –
http://www.ets.org/toefl/ibt/about?WT.ac=toeflhome_ibtabout2_121127

IELTS –

http://www.ielts.org/test_takers_information.aspx

THINGS TO CONSIDER

College admissions tests were listed by colleges as the third most important factor in the application process in the NACAC report, but like everything else so far, not all schools use test scores in the same way. It is important to understand what tests you have to take, when you should take them, and how the tests differ in an effort to increase your chances of getting in.

Additionally, the SAT (College Board) and the ACT have both announced that they will be offering revised versions of their tests:

http://www.nytimes.com/2013/08/04/education/edlife/what-the-new-sat-and-digital-act-might-look-like.html?pagewanted=all

If you are applying for admission for the fall of 2015, these changes will not impact your application. In fact, the SAT will not offer the new SAT until spring 2016. This means that in most cases, the students graduating in 2017 will be the first students with the opportunity to submit scores from the new SAT for admission consideration:

https://www.collegeboard.org/delivering-opportunity/sat/faqs

The ACT's new version of the test will be in digital format and will be available beginning in 2015 for schools who administer the ACT during the school day as a part of their required "assessment programs":

http://www.act.org/newsroom/releases/view.php?lang=english&p=2827

WHICH TEST IS BEST?

Many students ask, "Which test should I take?" A long time ago some schools did not accept the ACT for admission purposes. Your parents may remember this. However, that is no longer the case. All colleges and universities in the United States that require college admissions exams will accept either the ACT or the SAT. There is no penalty of any kind for submitting one score over the other.

Given the equal acceptance of both tests, it becomes a matter of personal preference. Perhaps the best strategy for test taking is to take both the SAT and the ACT in the spring of your junior year to see which one fits you best. Some students have a clear test preference as demonstrated in a stronger score on one test over the other. After you have taken both tests, you can compare your scores to see which test score is better:

http://www.act.org/solutions/college-career-readiness/compare-act-sat/

If you are not satisfied with your test score or feel you could improve your score with additional time and preparation, you can narrow your focus to one test or the other based on which initial score is higher. If your score is about the same on both tests then choose the test that felt most comfortable to you.

For students who are very strong in math and have taken an accelerated math curriculum, college admissions testing can be problematic. Specifically, the SAT only tests content in the areas of algebra I, geometry and algebra II. Students in a math class at or above pre-calculus/trigonometry in their junior year will not be testing on information they are studying in class. In contrast, the ACT tests math content from algebra I, geometry, algebra II, and trigonometry. Therefore, only students in Statistics or Calculus will be testing on information not currently covered in their math class. For this reason alone, some students choose their college admissions test based on their current math course placement.

Students in advanced math may wish to spend some time reviewing algebra and geometry before taking the SAT or the ACT so that they don't have to spend a great deal of time trying to remember how to do the basic functions on test day. Both the SAT and the ACT are timed tests. Students do not have the luxury of time to ponder every answer.

As a result of an accelerated math curriculum, some students choose to take the SAT in the spring of the year when they complete algebra II and take the ACT in the spring of the school year when they complete trigonometry or pre-calculus to get a strong math score recorded. There is one caveat to this approach – some schools require that you submit ALL of your test scores. If you are considering applying to very selective schools, you may have to submit all of your scores from all of the college admissions tests you've taken – SAT, SAT Subject Tests, and ACT. The College Board maintains a list of reporting requirements by school:

http://professionals.collegeboard.com/profdownload/sat-score-use-practices-list.pdf

It would be wise to check this list for any schools you are considering before you start your college admissions tests. If you are planning on applying to highly selective schools that require all test scores, it may be best to not take any college admissions tests (except subject tests that may align with your curriculum at an earlier time in high school) before spring of your junior year. Taking tests too early may actually detract from your application because of the trends that might become evident to such schools. For example, if you took the SAT in ninth grade and you retest at the end of eleventh grade and your score in a certain area drops or remains steady, it might send the message to the colleges that you haven't taken your curriculum seriously or that you have reached your maximum performance and may not have a strong potential to continue to grow academically. It is true that test scores are merely one aspect of the application, but they are one of the few ways that colleges can compare students on an equal playing field. It is always better to give colleges reasons to say "yes" than to give them data to justify a "no."

Additionally, if you took the SAT or the ACT while in middle school for a talent search or other high-ability program, it is critical that you check your testing accounts before submitting any test scores. Every year I have at least one student who submits his scores only to find out later that there was a test score from middle school included. The testing companies and the talent search agencies are supposed to be sure that these scores are removed, but sometimes scores get overlooked. It may not seem like a big deal if your middle school scores are included, however, they are not representative of your current achievement and can actually be detrimental to your application if they are misinterpreted because you took a college admissions test before you were academically, socially, or emotionally fully prepared to do so.

Submitting Scores

Both the SAT and the ACT give you the option of submitting scores for free to a certain number of colleges. If you are taking the college admissions tests for the first time in the spring of your junior year, you may not have a good sense of how you will do on the tests. While testing multiple times over the entire course of your high school career is not always the best choice, retesting in the late spring of your junior year or the fall of your senior year can significantly improve your application if your new scores are better. There is a charge to send your scores later, but for schools that only require one score, it might be to your benefit to wait and see which test score is the best and submit only that score even though it will cost you a little more. Many colleges say that they will use your best score regardless, but if they only have your best score (because they don't require all scores), there can be no misinterpretation of your score.

Another option that some schools offer is the opportunity to "super score" your tests. On the SAT this means that they will take your best sub-score from each test and add them together to recalculate a new composite score. On the ACT this means they will take your best sub-scores, add them together and divide them by four to create a new composite score. These scores are generally rounded up at 0.5 or above. So, in some cases, it could be beneficial to send more than one score if it gives you a better "super score."

Many schools will super score the SAT. However, while many schools will record your highest scores in each ACT content area even if they are from multiple ACT test dates, most schools will not calculate a new composite score. This means that you may get credit for raising your scores within the specific content areas, but you will not receive the benefit of a recalculated composite score across various test dates. And even more interesting, there are a very few schools that will actually super score between the two tests. It is to your benefit to know what the policy is for every school you are applying to so you can determine how to maximize your chances at each school. This may mean that you send different combinations of scores to different schools.

Finally, it is very important to realize that it is the student's responsibility to submit his test scores from the testing agency to the colleges where he is applying. Colleges will no longer accept test scores listed on high school transcripts. They must receive them directly from the ACT or the College Board. Students can request score reports online or by calling the testing agency. Fees vary based on method of request, but the online request is the most economical.

ACT

http://www.actstudent.org/scores/send/

SAT

http://sat.collegeboard.org/scores/send-sat-scores

Test Optional Schools

Many people believe that only two-year/community colleges will review applicants without requiring college admissions tests. However, there is a growing number of schools which will allow you to apply without submitting any test scores:

http://www.fairtest.org/university/optional

If you take a moment to review the list at Fairtest.org you will see that there are some competitive four-year schools on the list. These schools are commonly referred to as "test optional." Many times these schools have additional application requirements for students who choose not to submit their test scores. Certainly, if you have strong test scores and want to submit them to a test optional school, you can do so. Students with strong academic performance but mediocre standardized test scores are afforded the opportunity to demonstrate what they have learned in many different ways – essays, resumes, extracurricular activities, and additional teacher/counselor letters. The test optional school can open doors for students who might not otherwise be considered for admission because they don't perform well on standardized tests.

TEST FLEXIBLE SCHOOLS

An even newer concept is a flexible testing policy. Schools with flexible testing are also listed at fairtest.org. Test Flexible schools do require test scores, but they expand the list of tests to include more than the just the SAT or ACT. Test Flexible schools afford students the opportunity to choose the tests that best reflect their unique strengths. Most test flexible schools will accept subject test scores, AP test scores, or IB exams in lieu of the SAT or ACT. Students must submit test scores within the guidelines established by the college. For specific information about what tests are accepted, check the webpage for each individual college.

English Proficiency Tests

International students will have to submit English proficiency tests. The most commonly accepted tests are the Test of English as a Foreign Language (TOEFL) or the International English Language Testing System (IELTS). Some colleges waive this requirement for international students who have studied in a high school in the United States long enough or for students who score high enough on the verbal portion of the SAT. Again, school specific requirements can be found on individual college webpages.

In Review

- ✓ Develop a testing plan that considers your unique learning strengths and needs.
- ✓ Know what the testing requirements are for each school you are considering.
- ✓ Consider waiting to submit your test scores to colleges and universities after you have had the opportunity to evaluate all of your test scores.

Next Steps

Over the next several months or year, you will be asked to create many accounts to complete the application process. It can be overwhelming to try to keep track of all of the information that you will be required to create or report. Having all of your passwords in one place is a good way to keep things organized. It is important that if you choose to use a form to keep track of this information that you keep it protected so that others cannot access your accounts.

As you create accounts, enter your information in the table so that you will always be able to access your accounts.

Testing Passwords

Account	URL	Email	Username	Password
SAT	www.collegeboard.org			
ACT	www.actstudent.org			

As you complete the required tests, complete the table below to not only help you organize this information all together in one place but also to help you begin to formulate whether you need to complete additional testing before entering the college application process.

Academic - Testing

Assessment	Recommended test date	Date taken	Score	Retest : Y/N
PLAN	9th or 10th Grade		English = ____/34 Math = ____/34 Reading = ____/34 Science = ____/34 Composite = ____/34 Predicted ACT Range:	
PSAT	10th Grade		CR = ____/80 M = ____/80 W = ____/80 Composite = ____/240	
PSAT	11th Grade (NMSQT)		CR = ____/80	

			M = ____/80 W = ____/80 Composite = ____/240 National Merit Finalist Qualifying Score for my State:	
SAT	Spring Junior Year		CR = ____/800 M = ____/800 W = ____/800 Composite = ____/2400	
SAT	Fall Senior Year		CR = ____/800 M = ____/800 W = ____/800 Composite = ____/2400	
ACT	Spring Junior Year		English = ____/36 Math = ____/36	

A Simple Guide to Getting into College

ACT	Fall Senior Year		Reading = ____/36 Science = ____/36 Composite = ____/36 English = ____/36 Math = ____/36 Reading = ____/36 Science = ____/36 Composite = ____/36	
SAT Subject Test	Varies by subject		Subject: _____ Score: ____/800	
SAT Subject Test	Varies by subject		Subject: _____ Score: ____/800	
SAT Subject Test	Varies by subject		Subject: _____ Score: ____/800	
AP or IB (circle one)	Spring of course year		Subject: AP: ____/5 IB:	
AP or IB	AP = Spring of course		Subject:	

A Simple Guide to Getting into College

(circle one)	year IB = Spring Senior year		AP: ___/5 IB:	
AP or IB (circle one)	AP = Spring of course year		Subject: AP: ___/5 IB:	
AP or IB (circle one)	IB = Spring Senior year		Subject: AP: ___/5 IB:	
AP or IB (circle one)	AP = Spring of course year		Subject: AP: ___/5 IB:	
AP or IB (circle one)	IB = Spring Senior year		Subject: AP: ___/5 IB:	

CR = Critical Reading   M = Math   W = Writing

CHAPTER 3: CREATING YOUR LIST

KEY TERMS

Credit — A unit of measure related to the amount of time spent in college courses. A three-credit course would mean that a student would spend approximately three hours in class per week. At many colleges that implies that a student should be spending twice the amount of time out of class as in class to successfully prepare for the time spent in class. Many colleges require a minimum of 120 credits to complete a bachelor degree.

Major — The area of study in which you complete the most coursework for a bachelor's degree. The number of credits for a major varies depending on the college, but is generally at least 30 credits.

Minor — An area of study in which you complete a concentrated amount of coursework, but not enough to earn a major. The number of credits required also varies depending on college, but is generally at least 18 credits.

Middle 50% - Many schools report data from previous applicant pools. The middle 50% refers to the data of the students who were admitted in the middle of the class, or from the 25th to the 75th percentile. This data generally represents the average student admitted to the school.

Reach School – A school where it is very unlikely that you will be admitted based on your test scores, GPA, or intended major or because the school receives so many qualified applications that they simply cannot accept all qualified students.

Stretch School – A school where it is somewhat unlikely that you will be admitted based on your test scores, GPA, or intended major because your data falls just below the middle 50%, you are applying under a very popular major or college, or because the school receives so many qualified applications that they cannot accept all qualified applicants.

Likely School – A school where it is likely that you will be admitted because your test scores, GPA, and intended major are within the middle 50% or higher.

Solid Match School – A school where it is very likely that you will be admitted because your tests scores, GPA and intended major are at the high end of the middle 50% or higher.

Net Price – The federal government now requires all US colleges and universities to publish a "Net Price" for attendance:

https://nces.ed.gov/ipeds/resource/net_price_calculator.asp

This "Net Price" must take into consideration all of the costs and fees associated with attending a college as an undergraduate student seeking a first degree. Additionally, all schools must also have a "Net Price Calculator" available on their websites so that families may more accurately estimate the cost of attendance by entering family-specific financial information.

FAFSA – Free Application for Student Aid (www.fafsa.ed.gov). This is the document that students must complete to be considered for federal loans and grants:

http://studentaid.ed.gov/about

Expected Family Contribution (EFC) – An amount generated by the FAFSA:

http://www.fafsa.ed.gov/help/fftoc01g.htm

This amount captures what the federal government believes a family can afford to pay for college each year. It is important to note that the government bases this formula on spreading this amount over time even if it requires that the family take parent loans to pay this amount.

Dependent Student – Individuals who are considered "dependent" and must include parent income on the FAFSA unless he meets one of the following criteria: "at least 24 years old, married, a graduate or professional student, a veteran, a member of the armed forces, an orphan, a ward of the court, someone with legal dependents other than a spouse, an emancipated minor or someone who is homeless or at risk of becoming homeless:

http://studentaid.ed.gov/glossary#Dependent_Student

Graduate Assistant – A student who is studying at the graduate level who assists the PhD professors by teaching class, grading papers and tests, running labs, researching, or other academic tasks to allow the professor more time for research.

THINGS TO CONSIDER

Creating a list of schools to consider can be intimidating and overwhelming, but it can also be fun and exciting. This is your opportunity to explore as many of the more than 4000 schools in the United States as your time and resources allow. At the end of the exploration, you get to choose the schools that you believe will be a great place for you to continue your education.

CREATING AN INITIAL LIST

It is important to make sure that your initial list has both depth and breadth. This means that your list should have all four types of schools listed above (reach, solid match, etc.) as they relate to your specific needs. It also means that your list should take into consideration what type of financial aid you might need and what type of extracurricular activities you would like to have access to at the undergraduate level.

The first list you create should be large, especially if you are starting this process in your junior year. This is not the list that you will ultimately use to apply to colleges, but rather a list that you can use to, "shop around." It is important that you don't draw any lines in the sand at this point or refuse to consider options that might be a good fit for you. You may not see completely eye to eye with your parents on what schools should be on your list, so at this point in your search include all the schools that fit your criteria and your parents (especially if they are going to help fund your college education!).

You may be tempted to grab a college ranking list and start at the top and work your way down the list. However, that may not be the best approach to take as you begin your search. There are certainly many rankings available. Princeton Review, US News and

World Report, Colleges That Change Lives, and even Seventeen Magazine have published college rankings. Sometimes those lists include similar schools, but in many cases the lists look nothing alike. There is no consistent method used to analyze colleges. Each evaluator or group that publishes a list determines its own criteria. Some use faculty to student ratios as the most important criteria while others use the size of the endowment as the top indicator of college ranking. Your ability to interpret accurately these lists depends heavily on your understanding of their ranking criteria and the weight they assign to each individual characteristic.

For example, let's say that you have two friends who have been asked to write an article for your school newspaper on the best restaurants in your town. If "Friend A" loves pizza and eats it at least four times a week, his list is likely going to include several restaurants that serve pizza. If "Friend B" lives a vegan lifestyle, her list is likely to include many vegetarian friendly restaurants. While it is possible that one or two restaurants may appear on both lists, it is not likely that both lists will include all of the same restaurants in the same order. However, that does not mean that one list is right and the other wrong, it simply means that your friends have different tastes and their lists will reflect their individual preferences. It is not a bad idea to look at college ranking lists, but it should not be the only thing you use to determine which schools you are going to consider.

Here are several steps you can take to create a comprehensive initial list that reflects your unique interests:

1. Answer the following questions:
    a. If I had to choose a major today I would choose:
        i. _____
        ii. _____
        iii. _____
    b. I want to be:
        i. Close to home (within 100 miles or 2 hours by car)
        ii. Within my state or a neighboring state (within 300 miles or 5 hours by car)
        iii. Within a one-day drive (600 miles)
        iv. Far away (plane ride or multiple-day drive)
    c. I would consider:
        i. ☐ Yes ☐ No   Single gender school
        ii. ☐ Yes ☐ No   Military academy
        iii. ☐ Yes ☐ No   Religiously affiliated school
    d. The size of school that is most appealing to me is (undergrad only):
        i. Very Small (less than 2,000)
        ii. Small (2,000 – 7,500)

- iii. Medium (7,500 – 15,000)
- iv. Large (15,000 – 30,000)
- v. Very Large (more than 30,000)
- vi. Does not matter

e. I would like to have access to the following educational opportunities:
   - i. ☐ Yes ☐ No   Study Abroad
   - ii. ☐ Yes ☐ No   Participation in research
   - iii. ☐ Yes ☐ No Small class size
   - iv. ☐ Yes ☐ No   Majority of classes taught by PhD professors
   - v. ☐ Yes ☐ No   Internships

f. The following extracurricular opportunities are important to me:
   - i. ☐ Yes ☐ No   Performing ensembles
   - ii. ☐ Yes ☐ No   NCAA D1 Athletics
   - iii. ☐ Yes ☐ No Environmental clubs
   - iv. ☐ Yes ☐ No   Professional organizations (related to your major)
   - v. ☐ Yes ☐ No   Play a specific sport: _____
   - vi. ☐ Yes ☐ No   Other organized athletic teams
   - vii. ☐ Yes ☐ No Other Activities:
     1. _____
     2. _____
     3. _____

g. The location of my school should be:

    i. City (population of 100,000+)
    ii. Suburban (near a large city)
    iii. Town (population of less than 100,000)
    iv. Rural (away from major urban areas)
  h. My family can afford to pay:
    i. $10,000/year or less
    ii. $10,00 - $25,000/year
    iii. $25,000 - $40,000/year
    iv. $40,000+/year

2. Ask your parents the following questions:
  a. What type of job do you see me doing 10 years from now?
  _____
  b. How far away from home are you willing to consider allowing me to go?
    i. Close to home (within 100 miles or 2 hours by car)
    ii. Within my state or a neighboring state (within 300 miles or 5 hours by car)
    iii. Within a one-day drive (600 miles)
    iv. Far away (plane ride or multiple-day drive)
  c. What educational opportunities would you like me to experience:
    i. ☐ Yes ☐ No   Study Abroad
    ii. ☐ Yes ☐ No   Participation in research
    iii. ☐ Yes ☐ No   Small class size
    iv. ☐ Yes ☐ No   Majority of classes taught by PhD professors

        v.   ☐ Yes ☐ No   Internships
- d. What extracurricular opportunities do you think are important for me to consider:
    i. ☐ Yes ☐ No   Performing ensembles
    ii. ☐ Yes ☐ No   NCAA D1 Athletics
    iii. ☐ Yes ☐ No   Environmental clubs
    iv. ☐ Yes ☐ No   Professional organizations (related to your major)
    v. ☐ Yes ☐ No   Play a specific sport: _____
    vi. ☐ Yes ☐ No   Intermural athletics
    vii. ☐ Yes ☐ No   Other Activities:
        1. _____
        2. _____
        3. _____
- e. What size undergraduate enrollment do think would be best for me?
    i. Very Small (less than 2,000)
    ii. Small (2,000 – 7,500)
    iii. Medium (7,500 – 15,000)
    iv. Large (15,000 – 30,000)
    v. Very Large (more than 30,000)
    vi. Does not matter
- f. What can we afford per year for college?
    i. $10,000/year or less
    ii. $10,00 - $25,000/year
    iii. $25,000 - $40,000/year
    iv. $40,000+/year

A Simple Guide to Getting into College

3. Compare your answers with your parents and understand that your list should contain schools that meet your criteria and that meet your parents' criteria as well.
4. Complete a search for schools matching your criteria with the *National Center for Education Statistics'* College Navigator at http://nces.ed.gov/collegenavigator/ - click on the "More Search Options" tab to be sure to include all of your preferences. You may wish to search more than once with different criteria so that you can identify schools that are stretch, likely, and safety for you. You can also search for colleges for free at www.cappex.com, but you will have to create a student profile. The nice thing about the Cappex web page is that in addition to college searches it also offers a "What Are My Chances" calculator which will allow you to input your specific data and see how you stack up to students in recent admissions cycles. Another website that offers this information in a slightly different way is www.collegedata.com under the "calculate my chances" tab. Both websites provide useful information that may help you develop insight to what type of students certain schools are looking for, but neither site is the final authority on the subject. Perhaps you will want to check out both websites and decide which one provides the information in a way that is helpful and useful for you.
5. Create a list of the top 20 - 30 schools that meet your search criteria and identify them as reach,

stretch, likely, or safety. You may wish to do this in a spread sheet or table so you can easily track the schools and their specific criteria. By putting this data into a table, you will be able to see everything that is important to you in your initial search.

Campus Visits

After creating an initial list, it is time to start visiting campuses. The easiest way to visit campus is to take a "virtual tour." Most colleges have some type of virtual tour on their web page. It is possible you may be able to eliminate a few schools from your list based only on a virtual tour. As you take the virtual tour, ask yourself:

1. Could I see myself on this campus?
2. Do I like what I see about the academic focus of this school?
3. Am I interested in any of the things that are highlighted in the video?
4. Are there things outside of the classroom that interest me offered in this community?

If you answer "no" to all of the questions above, it isn't likely that you will fall in love with the school if you visit and you might want to eliminate it from your list. If you had more yesses than noes, it would be wise to schedule a time to visit the campus if your time and resources allow. Nothing can help you rule a school in or out more than a campus visit. It is your opportunity to see what campus life is like, taste the food (if you opt to eat on campus while there), see a dorm room, talk to a professor, view the athletic facilities, and talk to current students.

Many students believe they will have an "ah-ha" moment when they visit the "right" campus. However, for many students this simply isn't the case. Often, students find several campuses where they believe they could be very happy and successful. However, more often a student may leave a campus visit and know that she does not want to attend that school. This realization is very productive and will allow you to begin to reduce your initial list to a more manageable application list.

Many schools now have an online visit scheduling system. Check on the admissions page of the college and look for a "visit campus" or similar tab. Often you can personalize your visit by choosing what type of sessions you wish to attend. The information sessions are often directed by admissions office staff while campus tours are almost always led by current students. It is important to get information from as many sources as possible, so do both if possible. Additionally, some schools allow students to attend classes or spend the night on campus with a current student. Again, these experiences will allow you to gather more information from a variety of perspectives which will enhance your ability to decide if the school is a good fit for you.

After you have scheduled your visit using the online system or by calling the Admissions Office, be sure to confirm your visit a day or two before your scheduled arrival. Also before you arrive on campus you may wish to download the school's app for your smart phone or tablet. Many schools offer free apps which include driving directions, a map of campus, important student info, and sometimes even admissions tips.

On the day of your visit, choose your clothes wisely. Ripped jeans and a stained hoodie send a very different message than a clean pair of khakis and an ironed shirt. Everything is in play when it comes to your application and many admissions reps make note of even the smallest things. Dressing to make a positive impression is another type of demonstrated interest – it shows that you are genuinely interested and thoughtful about your college admissions process. Additionally, some colleges will do interviews for juniors during campus visits. In such circumstances, it is even more important to be dressed in appropriate clothing. It is also advisable to wear comfortable shoes because most campus tours are walking tours that last 60 to 90 minutes. If you need accommodations due to a physical limitation of anyone in your party, be sure to make the necessary arrangements in advance.

A Simple Guide to Getting into College

Plan to arrive at least 30 minutes prior to your schedule arrival time. Unless you've already been on campus multiple times, you want to leave yourself enough time to find visitor parking and walk to the Admissions Office or other location designated by the school. Again, a punctual arrival demonstrates that you taking your visit seriously.

During the info session the admissions staff will cover a wide variety of topics. You may wish to take notes during the information session so that you can remember what you have been told. After your second or third campus visit, the information will start to run together and you may not be able to differentiate the information from one school from another.

Often the presenters leave time at the end of the information session for questions. Here are some questions you can consider asking an admissions staff member if they are not covered in the admissions presentation:

1. Could you please share the top five things your college considers when reviewing applications for admission?
2. How important are SAT/ACT scores in the admissions process?
3. Do you consider AP Exam scores or SAT Subject Test scores when evaluating student applications?

4. How important are my extracurricular activities in the admissions process?
5. Should I tell you about my part-time job in my application?
6. Will additional letters of recommendation be helpful to my application?
7. What type of teacher (math, science, English, art, etc.) should I ask to write my letter(s) of recommendation?
8. Does your school consider the trend of my grades or just the overall GPA?
9. How important is my schedule my senior year?
10. Is demonstrated interest important at your school? What things do you consider as you evaluate my demonstrated interest?
11. I've heard that it's easier to get in if I apply Early Decision. Is that true at your college?
12. What decisions do you offer to your early applicants? If I'm deferred to the regular pool, does that pretty much mean I won't get in?
13. Do you prefer applicants who are well-rounded in multiple academic areas or those students who focus on just two or three?
14. What percent of undergraduate students are involved in research on campus?
15. Is it okay to say I'm "undecided" about my major on my application?
16. Do I have to apply to a particular school at your college? Or do I just apply to the college/university?
17. Do you typically take very many students from your Wait List?

18. Do you award merit scholarships in addition to need-based financial aid?
19. How do I apply for scholarships and financial aid?
20. Do you require a common core curriculum? If so, how many credit hours are required for the core?

The nice thing about campus tours is that they are most often led by current students. This is when you have the opportunity to ask the student what he really likes or doesn't like about the school from someone who is attending classes, eating on campus, and possibly living in the dorms. Here are some possible questions for the tour guide:

1. What do you like most about this campus?
2. If you could change one thing on campus, and money were no option, what would that be?
3. How many courses/credit hours are you currently taking?
4. What is the hardest class you've taken so far?
5. What about your high school experience most prepared you for your college coursework?
6. What do you do on the weekends?
7. How many hours a week do you spend studying?
8. How are roommates assigned?
9. What extracurricular activities do you do?
10. What other colleges did you consider/apply to? Why did you choose this one?

Narrowing Your List

With college visits complete, you can begin to narrow your application list. How you eliminate schools is a personal choice based on your preferences and priorities. If you have already eliminated some based on your experiences on campus, the next factors to consider might include cost, size, or curriculum.

Cost is a very real consideration for many families when it comes to deciding what school to attend. During the application process you are not deciding where to attend but rather where to apply. There is a big difference between the two. In many cases, parents and students rule out a school because they think it is too expensive. You will not know what type of financial aid and scholarships you are eligible for until your senior year, after you are accepted and after you complete the required financial aid documents. That is still months or years away. You will have to decide where to apply before you will know what your financial aid package will look like. However, there are some tools available to help you determine what an approximate net cost will be for each college you are considering.

If you look at the "Net Price Calculator" for each school on your list and you enter accurate financial information for your household, you can establish a pretty realistic price that your family will be expected to pay for you to attend. Some of the calculators are more helpful than others. Some are easier to understand than others. And, some are more accurate than others. However, these calculators can help you get closer to comparing apples to apples for the schools on your initial list. For a list of links to calculators for some of the nation's top schools, you can visit:

http://www.usnews.com/education/best-colleges/features/net-price-calculator

You can also find an average net price for each school and a link to each school's calculator on the College Navigator site cited earlier under the "Net Price" tab:

http://nces.ed.gov/collegenavigator/

The federal government requires students and their families to complete the Free Application for Student Aid or FAFSA to be eligible for federal grants and loans. From this application (www.fafsa.ed.gov) the federal government determines an Expected Family Contribution (EFC). The EFC is what most colleges use to determine what amount the student and his family can contribute annually to the cost of a college education. Schools that meet 100% of student need do not charge students more than their EFC. While most schools do not meet 100% of need, many do come close. The key piece that you need at this time is an estimate of your EFC. You can complete an estimate on the FAFSA website at:

https://fafsa.ed.gov/FAFSA/app/f4cForm?execution=e2s1.

Another form you might find helpful as you try to evaluate your net price and EFC is found at:

http://www.cappex.com/media/canYouAffordYourCollegeChoices.pdf.

In addition, the federal government provides many documents to help you understand the options available to students with permanent legal status or residence in the United States. These documents are all listed at:

http://studentaid.ed.gov/resources#information-on-getting.

If you do like rankings and lists, Kiplinger.com offers several "Best Value" lists for colleges. There are lists for private universities as well as public universities, but there are also other lists that may interest you such as universities with the worst graduation rates and college degrees with the best and worst return on investments. To see the various lists, search for "best colleges" on the Kiplinger.com main page.

After you head stops spinning from all of the financial talk, you might want to consider the size of the school as another important factor to use when evaluating differences between the schools on your list. Think about the type of student you are now and try to envision how your unique traits and characteristics will look once you are in college.

Imagine for a moment that it is Monday morning and you have an 8:00 class. You were busy all weekend and could really use some more sleep. Your 8:00 class is freshman biology in a lecture hall with over 300 students. No one takes attendance. You know that if you go, the professor will be at the front of the room racing through the lecture and you will be desperately trying to keep up, and your hand will be sore by the end of the class. Will you drag yourself out of bed to go to class even though no one will notice if you're not there?

Many large and very large schools also have large classes during the first two years. As a result, many freshman and sophomore level classes are taught in huge lecture halls with 300 or more students. Sometimes these schools have some type of break-out group later in the week where a graduate assistant reviews the material with students in smaller groups. If you are not likely to get out of bed to go to class, then a large university might not be the best choice for you because attending class is a critical component of academic success at the post-secondary level.

Small and medium colleges, especially liberal arts schools, tend to rely on more discussion-based classroom interactions. Some schools boast class sizes in the first two years of 30 or less. In these types of classroom settings it is very obvious when a student misses class and in many cases the professor of the class contacts the missing student to be sure she is okay. Sleeping in and skipping class is far less likely in such an environment.

While smaller schools offer a more personalized approach to learning, they sometimes lack the "rah" factor that is found at larger universities. If NCAA Division I-A Athletics are important to you, a small school won't be able to offer the same type of basketball or football as is found on the campuses of major universities across the nation. Additionally, small liberal arts schools often cannot offer the same variety of research opportunities or lab facilities because they have smaller budgets.

Certainly there are exceptions to these sweeping statements. There are a few small to medium schools with very successful Division I athletic programs. There are liberal arts schools with amazing labs and research opportunities, but until you visit the campus or more also provide a neutral review of your application portfolio and help you create a balanced list or they can give you an unbiased critique of your list with regard to admissibility. If you are interested in seeking outside support, here are some questions to ask that will help increase the likelihood that you will find a trained professional:

POSITIVE ATTRIBUTES

1. Does the consultant have any formal training or education in the area of high school guidance or college counseling or hold an advanced degree in the area of education?
2. Does the consultant hold any other licenses in related fields (school counseling, general counseling, school psychology)?
3. Does the consultant have multiple years of experience working in an admissions office of a school with high admissions standards?
4. Does the consultant offer career interest inventories or testing to help undecided students find majors and careers that might be of interest?
5. Does the consultant offer comprehensive services that begin early in the high school experience and continue throughout the application process?

Concerning Attributes

1. Does the consultant make promises or guarantees of Ivy League admission?
2. Does the consultant charge more than the average American's annual salary?
3. Does the consultant offer to complete applications for students or otherwise offer to help "fix" test scores that are too low?

Consultants who promise the moon or offer very limited services at significantly reduced prices may not be the best choice. Consultants who have advanced training or education in the field, however, have demonstrated an on-going commitment to working with adolescents and may better understand not only the admissions process but also the emotional turmoil it creates as you embark on the biggest decision of your life you have had to make so far. If in doubt about a person's qualifications, ask for references or ask about their experience and training in the area of college admissions counseling. A legitimate consultant will be able to provide one or both.

In Review

- ✓ Your initial college list should be filled with lots of schools that might be a good fit.

- ✓ Do your homework about schools by doing virtual tours, by visiting campuses, and by participating in info sessions at your high school.
- ✓ Families should not rule out a school based on the overall cost at this point in the admissions process.
- ✓ Remember that choosing a school is a very personal decision and one that should reflect your unique strengths, interests, and needs.
- ✓ Consider hiring a consultant if you feel that personalized attention will best serve your college admissions interests.

NEXT STEPS

Begin making your list of schools and completing campus visits. Develop a spreadsheet or other tracking device (see sample on the following page) so that you may begin to see similarities emerge that will allow you to highlight a specific type of school within your list. Be sure to include the data that is most helpful to you in your decision making process.

A Simple Guide to Getting into College

Name: John Doe
SAT Scores:
CR – 620   M – 750   W – 610
ACT Scores:
English – 30   Math – 35   Science – 32   Reading – 29
Composite – 32
GPA: 4.1 (4.0 scale)
Intended Major: Economics
Key: S = Stretch, R = Reach, L = Likely, T = Safety

School	State	SAT Range	ACT Range	Major: Y/N	D1 Ath: Y/N	Size	Study Abroad	Accept %	Status
Claremont McKenna	CA	650 - 750	28 - 32	Y	N	1,300	Y	14	S
Davidson College	NC	620 - 720	29 - 32	Y	N	1,750	Y	25	S
Harvard University	MA	700 - 800	31 - 35	Y	Y	10,000	Y	6	R
Indiana University	IN	510 – 660	23 – 30	Y	Y	35,500	Y	74	T
Northwestern University	IL	680 - 780	31 - 35	Y	Y	11,500	Y	18	R
UC San Diego	CA	520 – 710	23 - 32	Y	N	23,000	Y	35	L

University of Michigan	MI	610 - 760	27 - 34	Y	Y	27,500	Y	37	S
University of Rochester	NY	600 - 740	27 - 33	Y	N	5,600	Y	35	L

CHAPTER 4: THE APPLICATION

KEY TERMS

Common Application (www.commonapp.org) — An application which allows students to submit the same general application to multiple colleges and universities. There are currently more than 550 member institutions that will accept student applications via Common App. Some schools are exclusively Common App schools which means that the only way a student can apply to such institutions is via the Common App.

Universal Application (www.universalcollegeapp.com) — Another less frequently used application which allows students to submit the same general application to multiple colleges. There are more than 40 member institutions.

School Supplement — School-specific forms or essays required in addition to the common application.

Early Decision (ED) — A legally binding application to a college or university that is considered before the regular decision applications. Deadline for submitting most ED applications is November 1. Students who apply ED are generally notified by December 15 of their admission status. Students may only submit one Early

Decision application. And, if accepted to the ED school, the student is bound to attend that college as long as the student's financial need is met. In the early applications, the school has limited access to information regarding student financial need information because the FAFSA is not available until after January 1 of the senior year.

Early Action (EA) – A type of early application that is not legally binding, but allows students to submit their applications early and receive notification of their admission status earlier in the application cycle. Dates for EA applications vary more than ED applications, but generally the deadline to submit an EA application is early November. In most cases students can submit multiple EA applications. For many selective programs within schools, students are required to submit an early application to be considered for admission. Some schools, like Yale and Stanford, offer restrictive early action which means that students can only submit one early action application.

Regular Decision (RD) – A type of application which has no binding requirements. RD due dates vary significantly, but generally are not due before December 31/Jan 1 of the application year. Students are notified in the spring with a wide variance of notification between schools. This is the most frequently used type of application on the Common App.

Rolling Decision – Applications are processed as they are received. Students are notified of their status within a few months of submitting their application.

CSS Profile – An additional financial aid document required by many colleges and universities. This form is provided by the College Board and requires a fee to submit the profile to colleges and universities (student.collegeboard.org/css-financial-aid-profile).
This form captures additional assets and liabilities that are not captured by the FAFSA – including financial information from non-custodial parents.

THINGS TO CONSIDER

Once you have narrowed your list to a more reasonable number, it is time to get started on the applications. Many people debate what number is the "right" number of applications to complete. This varies from student to student. Some students feel very comfortable only submitting two or three applications while others want to have two or three schools from each category. And there are still others who want to submit two dozen or more applications. However, submitting a college application is not cheap – the average cost ranges from $50 to more than $100 per application. But perhaps more important is the fact that preparing more than six to ten applications may result in a lower quality application because of the number of essays and additional information that is required on the school-specific forms. If you choose to submit two dozen applications you will run the risk of looking mediocre on all of your applications instead of looking stronger on a fewer number of applications. In this case, more is definitely not better.

The NACAC State of College Admissions report for 2013 found that while a vast majority of students (77%) are still completing more than three applications, the number of students completing seven or more applications fell slightly to 28%:

http://www.nacacnet.org/media-center/PressRoom/2014/Pages/SOCA2013.aspx

This trend could prove to be a double-edged sword for students who are applying to college. On one hand, this trend may indicate that the majority of students applying to college are taking a thoughtful and informed approach to the process than in previous years which could, in turn reduce applicant pools at colleges slightly. But on the other hand, it could also allow students to spend more time on a fewer number of applications which might lead to a smaller but more competitive applicant pool. As data from additional application cycles become available, the implications of this recent trend may become more evident.

Finalizing your list of the colleges you will definitely apply to is just the beginning of the application process. The next thing you must decide is what timeline you should use to submit your applications.

When a school offers rolling decision applications it is almost always best to apply as early as possible in the fall. A rolling decision application means that the college evaluates each application as it is received and found to be complete. Once a program or college within the university is full, the remaining applications are denied, placed on a wait list, or sometimes offered admission to another program. The sooner your application is "read" the more likely you will be offered admission if you meet the minimum requirements.

The one time you might want to wait to submit a rolling decision application is if your grades in 11th grade were marginal or just below the admission standards for that particular institution, especially if there is a logical explanation to a slight dip in your junior year grades and the first semester of your senior year are stronger. Waiting to submit stronger grades from the first semester in your senior year could allow a college to say "yes" when they might have said "no" if based only on your grades through the end of your junior year.

For schools that offer early and regular application options it isn't quite as easy. There has been a lot of discussion in recent years about the boost an Early Decision (ED) application gives to students. The New York Times published a comparison of acceptance rates for early versus regular applications. The 2012 results and the 2013 results demonstrate a significant increase in the number of students choosing to submit an early application (2014 results were not published in this same format):

http://thechoice.blogs.nytimes.com/2012/04/16/college-admits-2012/

http://www.nytimes.com/interactive/2013/04/15/education/thechoice-2013-acceptance-rates.html/

In the many cases, acceptance rates in the early pool were twice as high as the overall acceptance rates. Specifically, as reported in 2012, Dartmouth accepted 25% of its early applicants but only accepted 10% of its overall applicants. Applying early does, in many cases, significantly increase your chances of being accepted. However, those increased odds come with some serious restrictions.

A student is only allowed to submit one early decision application. Under the Common Application, the student must confirm her commitment to the requirements of the Early Decision application by affirming the following:

> *"If you are accepted under an Early Decision plan, you must promptly withdraw the applications submitted to other colleges and universities and make no additional applications to any other university in any country. If you are an Early Decision candidate and are seeking financial aid, you need not withdraw other applications until you have received notification about financial aid from the admitting Early Decision institution.*

From the National Association for College Admission Counseling (NACAC) Statement of Principles of Good Practice:
http://www.nacacnet.org/about/Governance/Policies/Documents/SPGP_9_2013.pdf

> *'Early Decision (ED) is the application process in which students make a commitment to a first-choice institution where, if admitted, they definitely will enroll. While pursuing admission under an Early Decision plan, students may apply to other institutions, but may have only one Early Decision application*

pending at any time. Should a student who applies for financial aid not be offered an award that makes attendance possible, the student may decline the offer of admission and be released from the Early Decision commitment. The institution must notify the applicant of the decision within a reasonable and clearly stated period of time after the Early Decision deadline. Usually, a nonrefundable deposit must be made well in advance of May 1. The institution will respond to an application for financial aid at or near the time of an offer of admission.

Institutions with Early Decision plans may restrict students from applying to other early plans. Institutions will clearly articulate their specific policies in their Early Decision agreement.'

As you can see in the agreement, the only way to be released from the ED commitment, if accepted, is if you must decline based on a lack of adequate financial aid. However, ED applications are due in the first part of November, but the Free Application for Student Aid (FAFSA) isn't available until after January 1. So, the college must make an assessment of a student's need without the detailed information the FAFSA provides. Some schools use the College Board's CSS Profile to determine student need while others use their own formulas, but both are without the input of the federal financial aid form. Sometimes this process can take a while, especially if a student has unique circumstances.

If your family does not need to rely on a financial aid package to send you to a specific school, an ED application might be more appealing. But even if financial concerns are not an issue, it is important to understand that you are required to, "definitely enroll" if granted admission. If you haven't visited the campus and you are not certain that you want to go to a specific school, you shouldn't apply with an ED application. If you apply ED and you are accepted you will have to attend that institution for your first year. Period. It is that serious.

Another type of single-choice, early application is called Restrictive Early Action. According to the same NACAC document listed above, NACAC's Good Practice defines such applications as follows:

> 'Restrictive Early Action (REA) is the application process in which students make application to an institution of preference and receive a decision well in advance of the institution's regular response date. Institutions with Restrictive Early Action plans place restrictions on student applications to

> *other early plans. Institutions will clearly articulate these restrictions in their Early Action policies and agreements with students. Students who are admitted under Restrictive Early Action are not obligated to accept the institution's offer of admission or to submit a deposit prior to May 1.*

There is also Early Action that is non-restrictive. According to the same NACAC document listed above, NACAC's Good Practice defines such applications as follows:

> *'Early Action (EA) is the application process in which students apply to an institution of preference and receive a decision well in advance of the institution's regular response date. Students who are admitted under Early Action are not obligated to accept the institution's offer of admission or to submit a deposit prior to May 1. Under non-restrictive Early Action, a student may apply to other colleges.'*

Both types of Early Action applications aren't quite as serious as the Early Decision application, but they often do not produce any significant bump in acceptance rate unlike the Early Decision application does. However, for many programs that require auditions or portfolio review, students are strongly encourage or even required to apply EA so that their admission status can be determined before departmental status. This means that if you apply EA and are not admitted to the university, you won't be offered an audition. Many students apply to more than one EA school for this reason. Students also apply EA simply because they want to have an answer sooner. With the restrictive Early Action application, it will be important to weigh the benefits and drawbacks of limiting yourself to only one EA school when the boost from even the restrictive early application is negligible.

Take a look at your list of colleges where you will definitely be applying. Is there one school that you want to attend more than any other? Is there a school where you are just under the recommended admission standards? Is there a school that has net price calculator that makes the cost of tuition seem affordable for your family? If you answered "yes" to all three questions, an ED application might work to your advantage. It is important to include your intended time frame is for applying to each school – Rolling, ED, EA, or RD – on your final application list.

Once you have decided what type of application timeframe you have for each school, you are ready to begin completing the applications. Some schools have their own applications and will not accept any other application. Some schools have their own application and will accept the Common App. If you have the opportunity to fill out the Common App for more than one school, using the Common App can definitely save you time. Check your list of schools and see how many of them accept the Common App. Let's start there.

The Common App

The first thing you will need to do is create an account at www.commonapp.org. The Common Application released a new version of the Common App (CA4) on August 1, 2013 so it looked very different than it had in the past. The first year for CA4 was fraught with problems and difficulties for students, high schools, and colleges who were trying to use the application. As a result, several deadlines were extended. However, the Common App has redoubled their efforts to provide a fully functioning, glitch-free application for the 2014 – 2015 application cycle, therefore it is highly unlikely that application deadlines will be extended again.

With the CA4 you can create an account and see the types of information the Common App requires, even if you are a junior or younger. During the registration process you will choose a user name (email address) and password. Be sure you write these both down in a safe place! You will need both to log in several times in the upcoming months. If you are not a senior, you should choose "other student" in the account set up process. You will the following information to create your Common App account:

- ✓ Full legal name
- ✓ Email address (user name)
- ✓ Password
- ✓ Date of birth
- ✓ Mailing address
- ✓ Phone number

After you have created an account, you will be directed to the dashboard. There are four tabs – Dashboard, My Colleges, Common App, and College Search. There is also a help box within every tab that you can scroll through for additional help. You will want to go next to the College Search section to begin.

COLLEGE SEARCH

The College Search section is the place you will find all of the Common App member schools. Under the "Criteria" tab you can enter information to narrow your search, or look for Common App schools that have certain criteria such as miles from zip code, application deadline, or state. Enter as much information as you know about each school on your list. Once you have located a school that you wish to apply to, select the school and then choose "Add" to place the school to your application list. Once you have added a school in the Criteria tab, it will appear in your My Colleges tab. After you have added your schools, you can begin completing your application.

COMMON APP

The Common App tab has several subsections. You will need the following information to complete your application:

Profile

This section includes your demographic information, much of which will be auto-populated with the data you provided in the registration process. You will need to add additional details as they apply to you.

Family

You will be asked to provide a great deal of information about your family including your parents and siblings. The Common App now allows you to easily differentiate between parents that you live with and those that you do not. You will also need information about all of your parents' post-secondary education (if applicable).

Education

This section covers all of your high school education, dual enrollment courses, and future education plans. Be sure to report everything as accurately as possible as colleges will compare your self-reported information with the documents they receive from your school. You will also need your counselor's information including name, email address and phone number.

Testing

The testing section is another opportunity for you to self-report your scores. You can choose which scores you intend to send. As you select a test type from the list, boxes will begin to appear for you to enter your scores. Entering your information in this part of the Common App does not negate your responsibility to request official test scores from the testing agency, it simply allows schools to have an idea of your accomplishments on standardized tests are while they wait for verification from the correlating testing agency.

Activities

This is the place where you may list all of the amazing things you are involved with when you are not in class. However, you may only list 10 total activities from the duration of your high school career. For some students this is problematic. If you have more than 10 activities, narrow your list by including the ones that are most important to you, the ones in which you rose to leadership positions, or the ones that might closely relate to your intended major.

Writing

One of the major changes envisioned for the CA4 was that the essay questions would be different every year. However, the Common App announced that for the 2014 – 2015 application, the prompts would remain the same. It is unclear how many years they will reuse the same prompts, but generally speaking the Common App announces the writing prompts for the main essay in the spring for the application cycle that begins in August of any given year.

The CA4 also moved more requested information onto the school supplements so that the responses you enter in the general part of the application is truly "common" to all schools. It is very important to understand that the common portion of the Common App goes to EVERY SCHOOL. As you complete the application you will want to pay careful attention that you do not put anything in the general section that might show preference for one school over another.

The writing portion of the application also includes the disciplinary information section. In this area you must verify that you have never had any academic or legal infractions while in high school. If you find that you fit into a category that requires you to mark "yes" to either of the questions, it is important that you provide a reasonable explanation in the space provided. It would be prudent to have your counselor or another guidance/admissions professional review your response before you submit your application.

As you can see, the amount of required information is extensive. This application is not one that can be completed in fifteen minutes. But, once you have completed all of the questions on the Common App, you can print a preview of your application and you will have most if not all of the information you need for any other application.

My Colleges

Much of the information in My Colleges cannot be completed until you have entered all of the information in the Education tab of the Common App section. However, once you have entered all of the necessary educational data, it will "unlock" your access to the school supplements. While there are some similarities within each school tab, this is the part of the application that has the most differences. Within each school tab you can sign your FERPA agreement, assign recommenders, and access the school-specific information required before an application is considered complete.

FERPA Agreement

Before you can assign recommenders you must decide whether you will waive your rights to review the confidential letters of recommendation that were written on your behalf. In keeping with the family Educational Rights and Privacy Act (FERPA), you have the right to look at those letters after you turn 18 and enroll at a college. You must make a determination of whether you will waive your right to ever look at those letters. It is important that you read all of the information provided in the instruction part of this section of the Common App before you make your decision. If you choose not to waive your rights, many schools will not place as much value on your recommendations which could deter from your application.

Assign Recommenders

Your counselor will have to submit a reference on your behalf. You will also, in many cases, be required to ask one or more of your teachers for a recommendation. Teachers writing recommendations should be those who have taught you in either 11th or 12th grade. Some students immediately ask the teacher of the class where they earned the best grade, but this is not necessarily the best approach. The teacher who can most readily speak to your dedication, work ethic, or intellectual curiosity is not always the teacher/class where you earned the best grade.

A new addition to the CA4 is the ability for students to seek one additional reference from someone outside of the school. This means that your employer, clergy, travel coach, performing arts director, or other adult who has regular contact with you can provide a reference that may highlight an area of strength that your application might otherwise not include.

If your school uses Naviance, all of the recommendations must be completed through Naviance, so you will need to log into your Naviance account and request your recommenders through that website. You will not be able to assign or manage recommenders through the Common App because once you list your high school (which it knows uses Naviance) it will not allow you to add recommenders on your application.

However, if your school does NOT use Naviance, you will not only need to complete and submit your application but you will also need to manage your letters of recommendation by assigning them through the Common Application. Each recommender may complete the forms online or offline. If you do not enter an email address for your recommender you will then have access to the offline forms. However, if it is at all possible for your recommender to complete the online process it will expedite the receipt of your documents on the college side. All paper forms must be mailed to the college. Upon receipt, they must be scanned into an electronic format and then attached to your electronic application. This is a laborious process that can take several days at best if the forms are received by the college during the height of the application cycle. Additionally, in your student Common App account, you will only be able to see the status of your recommendations if they have been submitted electronically. The Common App does not update the status of any recommendations submitted offline.

The next three tabs – Submission Common App, Writing Supplement, and Submission Writing Supplement – under the My Colleges section relate to the submission of your application. Once you have entered everything and have reviewed and re-reviewed all of you answers in your Common App, you will be able to submit and pay for each application. You may wish to have your counselor, teacher, or parent review your application before you submit it. Once you send the application electronically you will not be able to make changes to the application (for that school). There is a process by which you can submit alternate forms of the Common App essay, but it is a bit cumbersome and you will be limited to a total of three changes over the course of

ALL of your Common App schools. To get the best results, you will want to be absolutely certain that everything is correct before you send your application to even one school.

When you finally submit your application under the "Submission Common App" tab, you are only submitting the common portion of your application. If a school has required information under the Writing Supplement section, and most do, you must also complete the Writing Supplement AND Submit the Writing Supplement for your application to be considered complete. In most cases this means that you must complete two submissions per school before the college can process your application.

For many students, one of the most troubling aspects of the Common App is that there is no phone support offered. As a result, all difficulties with the application must be reported via an online request. This can be incredibly frustrating for students who have blocked out time to work on the application but find that they are unable to proceed because of a technical difficulty. As a result, you may wish to plan several small blocks of time to work on the application in an effort to reduce your frustration should you run into difficulty.

On the Common App web page there is an explanation given for their decision to not offer phone support. The statement directly from the Common App is listed below for your review:

Why We Don't Offer Phone Support

Many applicants, parents, counselors, and teachers continue to call for phone support, and we understand why. Speaking directly to a support representative is an assurance that one's problems and frustrations are being heard and addressed. Unfortunately, given the volume of users who will interact with our system this year--well over one million, not including parents-- phone support would immediately become unsustainable. In addition, the system information that is transmitted when a user submits a request through our Help Center is often critical in helping us identify and solve the problem.

We assure you that every message submitted through our Help Center is evaluated by an individual member of our support team. These professionals work diligently to provide the most accurate and efficient assistance possible. There are times when the complexity of issues prevents them from responding as quickly as they or you would like, but they strive to provide the timeliest responses possible.

As you begin working on your Common App, it will be important for you to keep this in mind so that you do not find yourself stuck just hours before an application deadline. Many schools will not accept late applications and support for any difficulties is not a simple phone call away. If you cannot find an answer to your problem in the Help Center, you could wait for one or more days before receiving an electronic response.

SPECIAL APPLICATION GROUPS

International Students

Students that are applying from another country are often required to provide additional documentation. One of the forms most often requested is documentation of financial support. This form varies from one institution to another but is required to document that the student has access to enough financial resources to pay for his education. Some schools require this verification to come directly from a bank in the student's home country. Some require that the student verify financial support for one year while others require the student to demonstrate financial support for the duration of the degree program.

International students will also have to supply copies of passports and complete the correct visa application in the country of origin. While the college is responsible for a portion of this process, it is important to note that it is the student's responsibility to be sure that all required documents have been filed and processed before leaving his home to study abroad.

Student Athletes

Student athletes who are considering playing on athletic teams while in college face some additional application requirements depending on the level at which they hope to play collegiate sports. Students who wish to participate in intercollegiate athletics at NCAA Division I or Division II schools must complete the amateurism certification process through the NCAA Clearinghouse.

Initial eligibility is determined based on a combination of high school GPA and college admissions test scores which are documented through the Clearinghouse. The Clearinghouse uses a sliding scale to determine eligibility:

http://fs.ncaa.org/Docs/eligibility_center/Quick_Reference_Sheet.pdf

Students with high test scores have lower GPA requirements and likewise students with high GPAs have lower test score requirements.

The GPA reported by a student's high school is NOT the same as the GPA that the Clearinghouse uses to determine eligibility. Many high schools include most if not all grades earned by a student in their GPA calculations. The Clearinghouse does not. In order for a grade to be considered by the Clearinghouse, the course must be in an approved course. Each high school must submit course information for review and the Clearinghouse determines which courses will be accepted for amateurization certification purposes. Generally speaking, these courses fall in the core academic area. For a list of school-specific approved courses go to:

https://web1.ncaa.org/hsportal/exec/hsAction?hsActionSubmit=searchHighSchool

Another key difference between high school and Clearinghouse GPAs is the fact that the Clearinghouse does not administer a weighted GPA, but rather uses an unweighted GPA. In their calculations an A of any kind is worth four points. A B of any kind is worth three points, a C is two points, a D one point and an F is worth nothing. Student athletes can significantly increase or decrease their Clearinghouse GPA by making small changes. For example, if a student earns a C+ in a course it is worth two points but if she earns a B- it is worth three points. The difference between a B- and a C+ in a course is usually only a few percentage points higher, but when translated to the Clearinghouse GPA, those few percentage points can make a significant difference.

Student athletes may first create a profile once they begin their junior year of high school. After a profile is created, the student must submit official transcripts and test scores. The Clearinghouse will accept either a SAT or an ACT score, but the test scores must be submitted directly from the testing agency. Be sure that you are accessing the official NCAA documents and forms which can be found at:

http://web1.ncaa.org/ECWR2/NCAA_EMS/NCAA.jsp by selecting the Student-Athlete section

Whenever a student sends any information to the Clearinghouse Eligibility Center it is advisable to send it in such a way that delivery can be tracked and confirmed. They receive countless documents each year. If for some reason a document does not get attached correctly to your profile, a tracking number and date of receipt will allow them to more easily locate your documents.

Fine and Performing Arts Students

Have you considered majoring in musical theater, dance, voice, jazz, architecture, industrial design? These are just a few of the majors which require an audition, portfolio, or other supporting documents for admissions consideration. It will be important for you to be aware of these requirements and deadlines if you are applying to such a program.

One of the best ways to learn about the specific application requirements is to attend a fine arts college fair in ninth or tenth grade. NACAC sponsors such fairs regionally where hundreds of schools from around the country can be found in one location:

http://www.nacacnet.org/college-fairs/PVA-College-Fairs/PVAEXH/Pages/default.aspx

Many of the portfolio/audition/document requirements span the course of your high school career and it would be rather difficult to try to adequately document all four years of high school if you don't start keeping track of the necessary information until your senior year. This is definitely a time with starting in ninth grade is recommended. In the meantime, here are some ideas to get you started.

Art-Based Majors

1. Portfolios are the primary method for demonstrating your proficiency and growth over your high school career.
2. Portfolios are usually submitted electronically and are required to be include specific types of pieces of work as well as formatted according to specific instructions for upload. Portfolios usually include 12 – 20 pieces of your best work. Some of the types of work that are required by most schools:
   a. Drawings of real objects or observational drawings.
   b. Art work that reflects your personal style (this may be two dimensional or three dimensional work).
   c. Other documents may also be accepted as some schools encourage students to include anything creative that reflects personal philosophy or character as an artist. This can include other genres including essays, poems, musical compositions, or other original work.

Additionally, some schools may require specific types of work to be included. For example, the school may specify what one or more of the "real" drawings must be. To be sure that you have included everything necessary for each program you will want to visit the web page for each school and read carefully the portfolio requirements. To find more information on art-based schools or programs, visit www.artschools.com.

Music-Based Majors

1. In-person auditions are preferred and in some cases may be required. Many of the major performing arts programs offer both on-campus auditions as well as regional auditions.
2. A professional looking performance resume is highly recommended if not required at the time of audition. This should include :
    a. Instruments played/parts sung while in high school
    b. A repertoire of music you have performed over the course of your high school career
    c. Performing groups in which you have participated
    d. Professional or volunteer roles in which you have been cast while in high school (including pit crews or orchestras)
    e. Awards or recognitions related to your instrument/part

IN REVIEW

- ✓ Early Decision applications are legally binding, but they also provide a significant boost in acceptance rates.
- ✓ Early Action applications are not legally binding.
- ✓ The Common App has many parts to its application so don't wait until the last minute to complete it.
- ✓ Fine and performing arts programs have many additional requirements for an application to be considered complete.

NEXT STEPS

Begin completing your applications! Be sure to document all of your usernames and passwords as you create accounts. You may wish to create a spreadsheet or other document to store all of this information. A sample has been provided below:

Applications Used by Multiple Schools

Account	URL	Email	Username	Password
Common App	www.commonapp.org			

Universal App	www.universacollegeapp.com			

School Specific Applications

Name of School	URL	Email	Username	Password

CHAPTER 5: ESSAYS AND INTERVIEWS

THINGS TO CONSIDER

WRITING THE ESSAY

Writing the essay is often the most intimidating part of the entire application. But, it doesn't have to be. With a few simple steps you can write an amazing essay.

First, read the prompts from the Common App for the 2014 – 2015 application cycle which are available at Common App - Writing :

> *" The essay demonstrates your ability to write clearly and concisely on a selected topic and helps you distinguish yourself in your own voice. What do you want the readers of your application to know about you apart from courses, grades, and test scores? Choose the option that best helps you answer that question and write an essay of no more than 650 words, using the prompt to inspire and structure your response. Remember: 650 words is your limit, not your goal. Use the full range if you need it, but don't feel obligated to do so. (The application*

won't accept a response shorter than 250 words.)

- ✓ Some students have a background or story that is so central to their identity that they believe their application would be incomplete without it. If this sounds like you, then please share your story.
- ✓ Recount an incident or time when you experienced failure. How did it affect you, and what lessons did you learn?
- ✓ Reflect on a time when you challenged a belief or idea. What prompted you to act? Would you make the same decision again?
- ✓ Describe a place or environment where you are perfectly content. What do you do or experience there, and why is it meaningful to you?
- ✓ Discuss an accomplishment or event, formal or informal, which marked your transition from childhood to adulthood within your culture, community, or family."

If you are completing the Common App you will have to write on one of these topics. This is the essay that will be sent to every school on your list, so this is not the time to talk about how much you want to attend college "A." To get started, ask yourself: Which one of the above prompts seems like the best fit for you? Did a story or memory pop into your mind as you read one of the questions above? What about your experiences would appeal to all colleges?

If you can't decide which prompt is best for you, try brainstorming on all five of them. It will become evident which one you have the most to write about. But, here's the thing, you will only be allowed to use 650 words to answer the question. Another thing to consider as you evaluate the prompts is whether you can be concise enough to convey your thoughts about the topic in one page.

After you have listed ideas for all five essays, pick your strongest option. Keep in mind that there are certain topics it is best to avoid. Countless students write about their moms, dads or someone special in their lives. Don't! This essay isn't supposed to be about your mom or any other person for that matter. It is supposed to be about YOU.

Not only is your essay supposed to be about you, it also needs to be written in your own voice. It is normal and even expected for your parents to want to help you write your essay, but be careful that it doesn't become their essay instead of your own. The people in college admissions are very good at evaluating whether the application really reflects the student's work or whether he had a lot of help from outside sources. This is why it is so important that the topic you choose needs to feel right to you. If you are struggling with finding your voice, check out the WOW Writing Workshop Webpage for some tricks to get started (www.wowwritingworkshop.com).

Some of the best essays I have read have been written about shoes, mosquitoes, mowing the grass, or pizza. Every year I have at least one parent who calls me in a panic because he is certain that his child's essay is written on "the most ridiculous topic!" But a well written essay about pizza can be incredibly compelling and catchy.

With that in mind, think about the story you want to tell. What image first comes to mind? Is it something that actually happened, a story you have read, a place you have visited, or perhaps it is something you would like to do. Imagine yourself taking a picture of the thing, place or event. Don't wait, start writing! Describe the picture you just took and make sure you capture every detail.

Now, read what you have written. Does it make sense to you? It is important to consider your intended audience for this essay. Many students imagine a staunch, gray-haired man sitting behind an enormous desk reading essay after essay and marking the files with a rubber stamp "admit" or "deny." However, the reality is that most applications are first read by an admissions representative. Search a few admissions web pages and you will quickly see that many of the admissions reps have just recently graduated from college themselves. They are often in their 20's or early 30's. They are not too far removed from their own applications and they have a very good understanding of all of the tricks students may try to avoid the agony of writing an essay for a college application. But the most important part of the essay is allowing the college to hear your voice.

Back to the description you just wrote. Make sure you include some tantalizing details. What do you see, hear or feel as the scene unfolded? You want something in your first few sentences to hook your reader – the 20 or 30-something college admissions rep who has to read thousands of essays with every application cycle. If you had to read that many essays, would you be exited to keep reading an essay that starts, "I recently traveled to Ghana on a mission trip?" NO! But what about an essay that started, "The ground cracked into a million tiny pieces in the heat of the raging sun. I could feel the sweat dry on my skin as quickly as it formed..."

Once you start writing, don't stop. It is important to be sure that you get all of your ideas down on paper. Your first draft might be 1000 words or more, but that is okay. By writing more than you need, you will have the freedom to edit out the information that ends up be superfluous. Eventually the hook will end up being the first one or two sentences of the first paragraph. After you have your hook, move immediately into the details about the how, when, or where of your story. What actually happened? Be sure to continue to tell your story in a way that the reader can actually visualize the scene.

The second part of your essay should focus on the "take-aways" you have learned as a result of this experience. What immediate lessons did you learn as a result of that experience, place, or activity?

The final part of your essay should focus on the long-term applications you have made as a result of the experience you described at the beginning of your essay. Specifically, think about the following questions and provide an answer to at least one of them:

- ✓ How are you different today as a result of what happened?
- ✓ How do you interact with the world around you now as a result of this experience?
- ✓ What things would you like to change or continue to change as a result of this event?
- ✓ How will you do things differently in the future as a result of this experience?

Colleges have more qualified applicants than they have seats in their freshmen classes. They want to choose someone who is going to bring her strengths to the campus and share them with others. It is important that you give the college a reason to keep you in the "yes" pile. A compelling essay can do that for you.

Once you are done, your essay should include:

1. A hook
2. A description of the how, when, where of the story
3. A explanation of the lessons you learned as a result of this experience
4. A reflection on how you are different as a result of this experience

If you have all four parts, your first draft is done. The best way to improve writing is to let it rest for a while before returning to work on it again. If time allows, leave it alone for at least a week. Some additional resources to continue if you are still stumped are:

http://www.nacacnet.org/studentinfo/articles/Pages/Top-Ten-Tips-for-Writing-a-College-Essay.aspx

When students are stuck they often ask me for samples of essays from other students. Certainly there are a ton of examples online and, on occasion, reading examples helps a student get "unstuck." However, more often than not, students try to emulate the essay that they liked the most and once again, their voices get lost in the story of someone else. It cannot be underscored enough that this needs to be your own story in your own voice.

After you have written and rewritten your essay, it is time to have someone else read it. Make sure you have checked it for grammatical errors and have proofed it at least once before you ask someone to donate their time reviewing your essay for you. While your friends might really want to read it for you, I would encourage you to find a trusted adult to take a look at it. An English teacher, or a college or guidance counselor at your school might be able to provide you with the most meaningful feedback.

Congratulations! You have completed your essay! It is likely that you will have more essays to write for the school supplements. As you continue to write more essays, try to include a hook and a personal reflection as you address the prompts.

Preparing for the Interview

After you submit your application, you may be contacted for an interview. Many selective schools suggest and some even require an interview. Institutions have as many different procedures for interviews as there are types of cars on the road. Sometimes they have alumni conducting regional interviews. Other times they have the admissions rep meet the student for the interview. And, still other times they conduct interviews on campus if the student requests one when scheduling a campus visit.

Many students obsess over lists they have found online of possible interview questions. They rehearse answers and memorize impressive facts they hope to interject at some point, but that isn't the point of the interview. Much like the essay, the most important aspect of the interview, regardless of who is conducting it, is for you to be yourself. College reps, alumni, or students who conduct interviews are savvy people. They will recognized coached or memorized responses. As you prepare for your interview, instead think about yourself. For example, consider the following questions:

1. What three words would you use to describe yourself?
2. What is your most favorite leisure activity? Why?
3. What three words would your best friend use to describe you?
4. If you were given a large sum of money, how would you spend it?
5. If you could change one thing about your community, what would it be? Why?
6. Where do you see yourself 10 years from now?

It is okay to say that you don't know the answer to a particular question. It is okay to laugh, and it is okay to be nervous. But even though the interview can be intimidating, try to relax and let the person on the other side of the table have an opportunity to see the unique person you are.

IN REVIEW

- ✓ A strong essay includes a hook, a description, and a reflection.
- ✓ Be sure to proofread your essay.
- ✓ Check the word count on your essay, you will not be able to submit more than 650 words.

CONCLUSION

Once you've visited campuses, chosen schools that best fit you, written your essays, submitted your application, and participated in interviews, there is nothing more you can do but wait. Perhaps, that is the hardest part of the whole process. Waiting. Dr. Seuss may have captured it best in, Oh, the Places You'll Go!, when he wrote about how useless it feels to be stuck waiting. But take heart, the waiting will come to an end.

You did your research and applied to a balanced list of schools, and as a result of your hard work there will be a great place for you after you graduate from high school. You will find a great fitting college that is excited to have you as part of its entering class. If you read all of Dr. Seuss' words in Oh, the Places You'll Go!, you just might come to the conclusion that it is the journey and not just arriving at your destination that brings the greatest satisfaction.

So, what are you waiting for? Get going!

ABOUT THE BOOK

A Simple Guide to Getting into College has been designed to help you navigate the admissions process without feeling overwhelmed. Each year this book will be updated to reflect the most recent statistics, trends, and advice for students submitting college applications in the upcoming year. If you would like to share any suggestions for upcoming editions, please email your ideas to info@SimpleGuidetoGettingIn.com.

ABOUT THE AUTHOR

Heather Case works full-time as a college counselor at an independent school in Indiana. She has worked with children, adolescents and their families for nearly two decades. She also works with students and their families as an independent consultant. For more information, please visit:

www.SimpleGuidetoGettingIn.com.

A Simple Guide to Getting into College

OTHER SERVICES AVAILABLE AT WWW.UDEMY.COM

SGTGI: Understanding the Admissions Process

SGTGI: Preparing for the Admissions Process

SGTGI: Completing Your College Applications

SGTGI: Writing an Effective Common App Essay

SGTGI: The Complete College Admissions Suite

Use the following coupon code to get 50% off any class:
I READ THE BOOK!

Simple Guides

give you

Just the Facts

GET UP TO SPEED ON THESE TOPICS—FAST!

Simple Guides: get you started quickly. No extra clutter, no extra reading. Go to

www.luminisbooks.com/category/topics-of-interest

Isbn: 978-1-935462-64-4

Isbn: 978-1-935462-68-2